PIXAR FOR PIANO

ARRANGED BY KEVIN OLSON

Disney/Pixar elements © Disney/Pixar

ISBN 978-1-70516-636-9

Visit Hal Leonard Online at
www.halleonard.com

World headquarters, contact:
Hal Leonard
7777 West Bluemound Road
Milwaukee, WI 53213
Email: info@halleonard.com

In Europe, contact:
Hal Leonard Europe Limited
42 Wigmore Street
Marylebone, London, W1U 2RN
Email: info@halleonardeurope.com

In Australia, contact:
Hal Leonard Australia Pty. Ltd.
4 Lentara Court
Cheltenham, Victoria, 3192 Australia
Email: info@halleonard.com.au

From the Arranger

A motto at Pixar Animation Studios is "Story is King." Whether it is the dialogue-free opening montage of Carl and Ellie's married life in *Up*, an average day of garbage-collecting by a robot in *Wall-E*, or the inner workings of an 11-year-old's brain in *Inside Out*, Pixar's mastery at creating stories have continued to emotionally resonate with audiences of all ages for over 30 years.

A crucial tool in this masterful storytelling process is the work of incredible film composers like Randy Newman, Michael Giacchino, Thomas Newman, and others. This collection of arrangements focuses on the wonderful music that support Pixar's storytelling in dramatic and powerful ways. Each has a distinct mood that should be reflected in pianists' performances, and offers challenges to intermediate and early advanced pianists in rhythm, phrasing, and tone color. They are designed for both solo recitals and as mood-setting music to weddings, receptions, and other events.

I hope you enjoy telling these classic Pixar stories all over again with your own expressive performances, taking them "To Infinity and Beyond"!

Kevin Olson

Kevin Olson is a pianist, composer, and member of the piano faculty at Utah State University, where he teaches piano literature, pedagogy, accompanying, music theory, commercial composition, and rock & roll history, among others. Dr. Olson coordinates the piano program at Utah State, and oversees the Utah State University Youth Conservatory, which provides piano instruction to over 150 pre-college community students. A native of Utah, he began composing at age five. He has written music commissioned and performed by groups such as the Five Browns, American Piano Quartet, Chicago a cappella, and the Rich Matteson Jazz Festival. In addition to maintaining a large studio of students with varying ages and abilities, he has also presented workshops and performed nationally as well as in India, China, Canada, and the United Kingdom.

CONTENTS

BUNDLE OF JOY
from INSIDE OUT

By MICHAEL GIACCHINO
Arranged by Kevin Olson

Sweetly, not too fast

Weightless; a bit slower

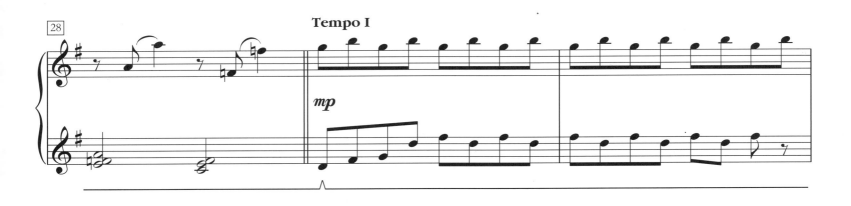

Tempo I

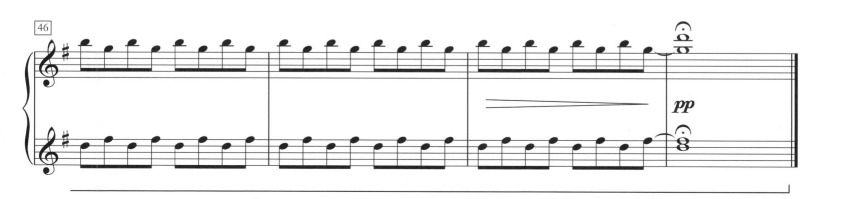

DOWN TO EARTH
from WALL-E

Music by THOMAS NEWMAN
and PETER GABRIEL
Words by PETER GABRIEL
Arranged by Kevin Olson

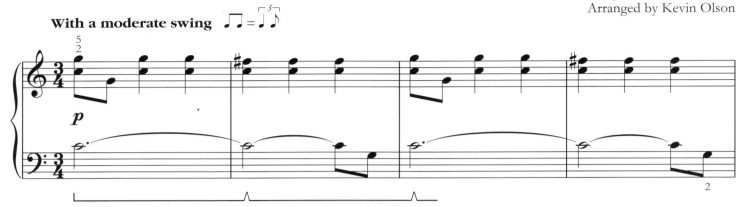

IF I DIDN'T HAVE YOU

from MONSTERS, INC.

Music and Lyrics by
RANDY NEWMAN
Arranged by Kevin Olson

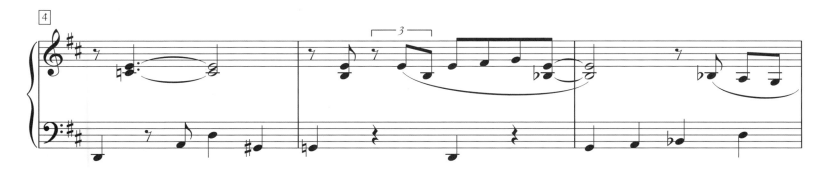

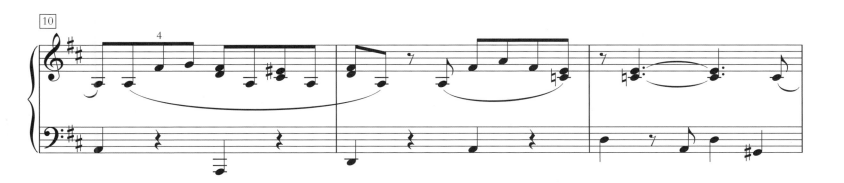

THE INCREDITS
from THE INCREDIBLES

Music by MICHAEL GIACCHINO
Arranged by Kevin Olson

IT'S ALL RIGHT
featured in SOUL

Words and Music by
CURTIS MAYFIELD
Arranged by Kevin Olson

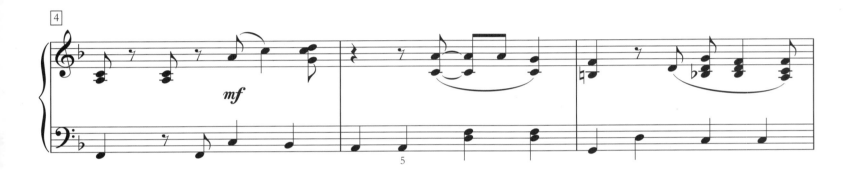

MARRIED LIFE
from UP

By MICHAEL GIACCHINO
Arranged by Kevin Olson

Lightly and moderately fast

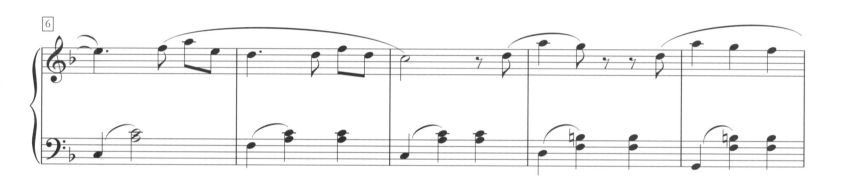

LAVA
from LAVA

Music and Lyrics by
JAMES FORD MURPHY
Arranged by Kevin Olson

Moderately slow

LIFE IS A HIGHWAY

featured in CARS

Words and Music by
TOM COCHRANE
Arranged by Kevin Olson

Quickly

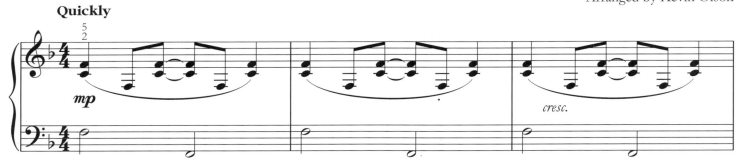

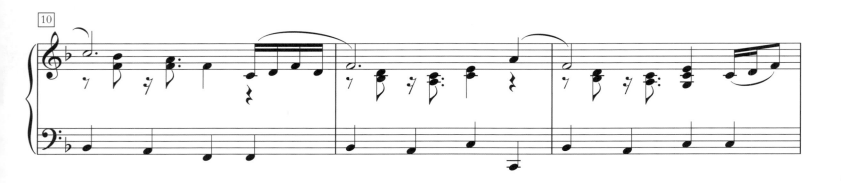

NEMO EGG
(Main Title)
from FINDING NEMO

By THOMAS NEWMAN
Arranged by Kevin Olson

Floating; weightless

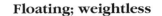

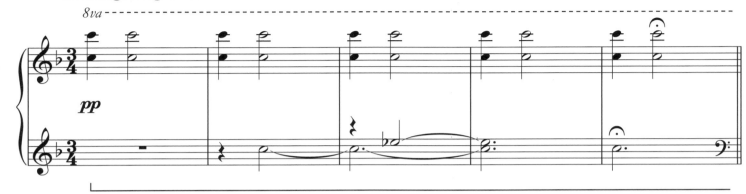

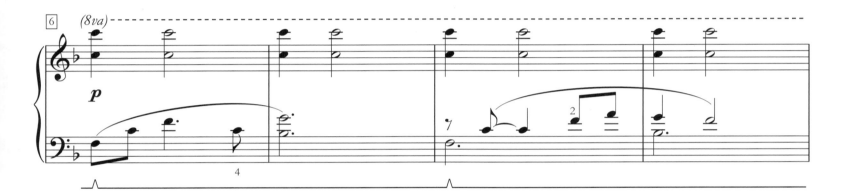

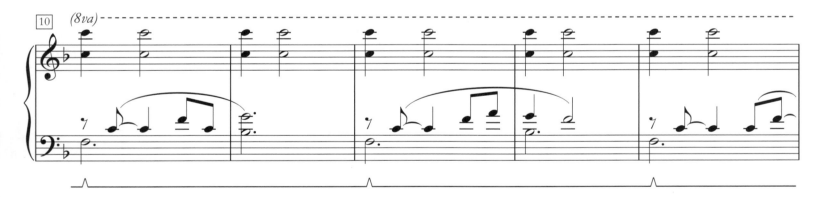

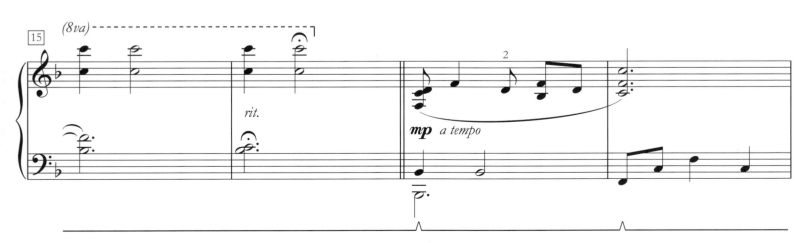

RATATOUILLE MAIN THEME
from RATATOUILLE

Music by MICHAEL GIACCHINO
Arranged by Kevin Olson

Slowly and expressively

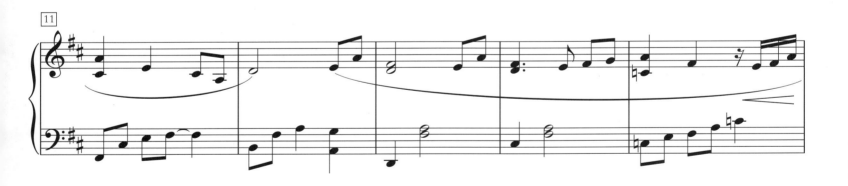

REMEMBER ME
(Lullaby)
from COCO

Words and Music by KRISTEN ANDERSON-LOPEZ
and ROBERT LOPEZ
Arranged by Kevin Olson

WHEN SHE LOVED ME
from TOY STORY 2

Music and Lyrics by
RANDY NEWMAN
Arranged by Kevin Olson

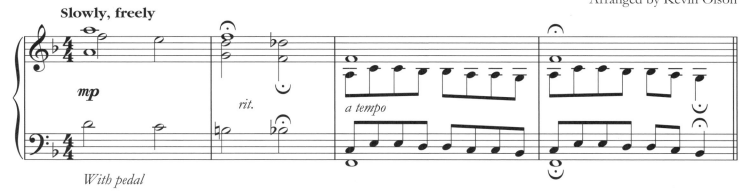

THE TIME OF YOUR LIFE

from A BUG'S LIFE

Words and Music by
RANDY NEWMAN
Arranged by Kevin Olson

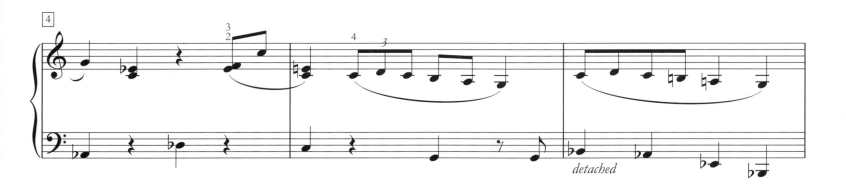

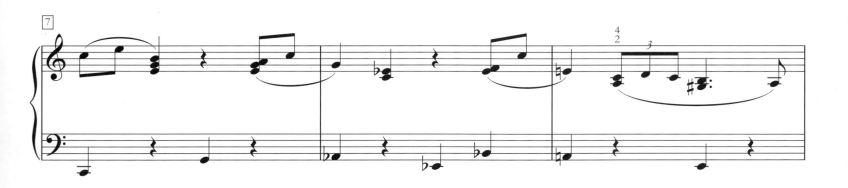

TOUCH THE SKY
from BRAVE

Music by ALEXANDER L. MANDEL
Lyrics by ALEXANDER L. MANDEL
and MARK ANDREWS
Arranged by Kevin Olson

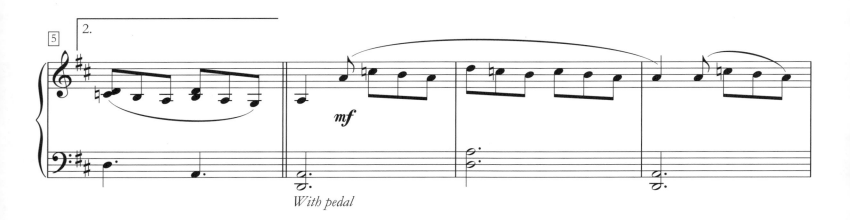

YOU'VE GOT A FRIEND IN ME

from TOY STORY

Music and Lyrics by
RANDY NEWMAN
Arranged by Kevin Olson